PENSUPREME®

PENN DAIRIES, INC.   1801 Hempstead Road, P.O. Box 7007, Lancaster, Pa. 17604   717-394-5601

John F. Garber, Jr.
Chairman of the Board and
President

Dear Friends:

My family's roots in Lancaster County, Pennsylvania are
deep, firm, and, if you'll excuse a bit of pride, they've
borne rich fruit.

Our family history tells us that Christian Gerber obtained
a deed for a 236 acre tract of farmland in July of 1741.
At some point in the ensuing years, one of my forebears
made a slight change to the spelling of my family name.
One thing that hasn't changed, however, is our connection
to the land, through the primary product of Lancaster's
farmland - milk and dairy products made with milk.

My grandfather, Eli Lindemuth Garber, opened the business
which was to become Penn Dairies in 1890. His vision
was to serve the community with exceptional quality dairy
products. His vision became reality, and today, our
company serves Lancaster and surrounding communities with
a full range of nutritious dairy foods.

Lancaster is recognized for its many characteristics: its
lush farmland, its tranquility, its distinctive quality
of life, and for the Amish who are such an integral part
of its charm and its soul.

The Amish people--their strength of community, their hardy
work ethic, and their engaging personalities--are celebrated
and brought to life by Ruth and Blair Seitz in "Amish Country."

We're privileged to be their neighbors, and we take pride
in providing you with "The Fresh Rich Taste of Lancaster
County" through our Pensupreme dairy products.

Thank you for permitting us to share our pride with you.

Sincerely,

John F. Garber, Jr.

AMISH
COUNTRY

CLB 1706
© 1988 Colour Library Books Ltd.,
    Godalming, Surrey, England.
All photographs © 1988 by Blair Seitz.
Printed and bound in Barcelona, Spain by Cronion, S.A.
All rights reserved.
This edition published 1988 by Crescent Books,
    Distributed by Crown Publishers, Inc.
ISBN 0 517 67361 4
h g f e d c b a

DEP. LEG. B-30.710-88

AMISH
COUNTRY

by Ruth Hoover Seitz
Photography by Blair Seitz

CRESCENT BOOKS
NEW YORK

Preface

My beginnings were here in this fertile basin of Lancaster County in southcentral Pennsylvania. And this was also my ancestral home, the birthplace of my parents and grandparents and great grandparents. Among my Mennonite family memorabilia is a farm deed signed by William Penn's son Thomas.

Mennonites share much European history with the Amish. My roots became a route to relationships with Old Order Amish, especially those who knew my grandfather. And within those friendships I experienced Amish rhythms and learned their significance as well as appreciating their meaning.

To safeguard their privacy, I have promised all persons that I would hide their identity. The names used are realistic but not actual. Some details are interchanged for anonymity.

I am grateful to several organizations that shared their facilities and services: the Mennonite Information Center, the Pennsylvania Dutch Visitors Bureau, The Amish Homestead, Witmer's Inn and the Pequea Bruderschaft Library.

Blair and I appreciated the hospitality and helpfulness of my parents as we shaped this text and these images into a unit.

Beyond my seat on a rock the landscape rolled out neatly-defined fields of earth brown, alfalfa blue, and soft green corn frills. Like a quilt, the strips of land bent with the contour of the mass underneath. This spring patchwork is Pennsylvania's eastern Lancaster County, some of the richest farmland in the United States.

But people around the world also know this area as the home of the Old Order Amish, a people who till their land and direct their lives with faith, simplicity and ardor. Because their lifestyle resembles the eighteenth century more than the twentieth, they are distinctive. I looked across the fields for some images that characterize these religious people.

Their neatly painted farmsteads dotted the countryside. Near most houses rose a windmill, its spinning wheel a contrast to the angular fields. No electric wires ran from their barns, tobacco sheds and houses standing crisp in the morning light. White wooden fences instead of electric wires kept the cows in the meadow. A horse clip-clopped against the macadam, a pleasing staccato in the still morning. It pulled a gray-covered buggy, their family vehicle. In one pasture several other horses rolled on their backs. The scene before me was free of the clutter of technology and radiantly silent.

In one Amish yard I spotted an apartment birdhouse that could accommodate 24 families of purple martins. These communal birds return each spring to the same house to raise a new family. The martins were swooping to and fro, no doubt catching insects. Amish in various states have respected the martins by building houses to their liking. The two groups share the need to live near their own.

The mint leaves I saw growing in the meadow of the first farm brought back the hospitality I enjoyed during a summer barn-raising.

The sun was now higher. Dairy farmers had finished the milking. Cows were going to pasture, and a few diesel engines started humming to cool the milk in bulk tanks. Two straw hats were moving from a milkhouse, the men on their way to breakfast. Wash was appearing on lines that moved by pulley from house to barn. I knew that children wearing the same solid colors flapping from the washline would soon walk in groups towards a bell-topped schoolhouse.

A black carriage moving in the distance, the style of the Old Order Mennonite, reminded me of the other "plain folks" who live here, some formed from splits on practices but still tracing their origins to Europe.

The 15,000 Old Order people here represent the oldest of Amish settlements in 20 U.S. states and one Canadian province. There are about 46,000 in all. Interestingly enough, there are no Old Order members in Switzerland or Germany, from where the first migration came to the U.S. in the 1720s.

The largest group lives in Holmes and Wayne Counties in Ohio, the destination of a second migration from Europe in the 1800s. According to historian David Luthy, the Amish population nearly doubles every twenty years. Seventy per cent of 188 total settlements were founded since 1960. An average of seven new settlements are founded each year.

The Farm Home

When the first wave of Amish accepted the invitation of William Penn's sons to settle in Pennsylvania in 1727 they looked for land with mature trees, assuming it would be well-watered. They had their eye on fertile land that would yield for their sons and grandsons despite the immediate struggle of clearing large trees.

The tasks of the farm demand full-time input from the whole family. While caring for the crops and animals, parents are able to show children how to live and make a living without exposure to influences that would confuse or contradict their beliefs. In this way, the farm becomes a setting for religious nurture as well as an enterprise that provides for the basic needs of the family members. This culture has operated on the epithet, "The family that plows together stays together." The staying means religious commitment in the terms that the Amish community has set.

There are strong sentiments on the use of land, time and energy because the Amish believe these resources are gifts of God. They view the land as a source of nourishment for people and take care of it to maximize its productivity. It would be unthinkable to refrain from planting a field for government subsidy. And also to neglect a difficult task that would improve the soil's fertility. To this end, Amish farmers seek modern agricultural information.

Time, especially daylight time, is important as an opportunity to care for the family and the land. An Amish farmer depends on the sun more than any other energy source. As long as the sun is up, there is a chance to plow a straight furrow or cut tobacco. But a lantern can light the confined space of the barn for farmers to milk the cows before dawn. In many families the schoolage children are roused between four and five in the morning to help with the milking before breakfast and classes. Evening darkness is a time for slowing down; for gathering the family under the single artificial light, usually a propane gas lamp, and retiring early.

An Amish home uses limited fossil energy. The kitchen lacks electric-powered appliances. The stove and fridge have been converted to use bottled gas. Floors require sweeping and washing rather than vacuuming. Women and girls master a treadle sewing machine that usually stands in front of a well-lighted window.

There is no TV, radio, VCR or computer. In fact, there are no electrical outlets. Avoiding the source of power rules out the temptation to use it for forbidden entertainment. Years before TV, the Amish had already rejected electricity because maintaining the system required people to break the Fourth Commandment by working on Sunday rather than keeping it holy.

Instead of switching on a light at one's convenience, an Amish household and schoolroom operates primarily by daylight. On gray days I have been in poorly lit rooms, but work continued without any artificial light.

Because of the time involved in lighting a propane lantern and the safety of keeping it at one place, family members move toward the kitchen light to sew, read or write letters. Under parental eyes, children are likely to read acceptable material. The absence of a central heating system also draws the family together during evening time.

In the heat and warmth of the kitchen, members grant each other privacy within their togetherness. The other evening Joe Esh and I were discussing farm practices under the mantles of a gas lantern in his kitchen. His wife Lizzie sat at the same table, lost in her crossword puzzle. Here, with no other illumination, the hissing lamp drew us inside an enclosing brightness.

When Joe mentioned that he takes the propane container to the Coleman center for refilling every ten days or so, I mentally noted this Old Order chore replaces running for new lightbulbs.

An Amish farm owns at least six horses and mules to pull field implements for cultivation and four driving horses. These animals must be fed and sheltered year-round, but they also produce soil-building manure. Joe tugged his white beard, explaining the benefits of this natural fertilizer. "We spread more manure than non-Amish farmers because we have it. Its high nitrogen content means that our soil needs less of that mineral in commercial form. Also, the straw makes manure effective for a longer time than liquid fertilizer which tends to leach away."

Amish farmers feel that straw and their cultivation methods aerate rather than compact the soil. Well-drained soil can be ploughed early.

Joe hooked his thumbs in his suspenders and continued talking about the economic virtues of draught power. "A three-year-old workhorse will be worth a third more than what I bought it for after three years of solid training and muscle-building. However, a $30,000 tractor starts to depreciate as soon as it is delivered."

The farm implements of the Old Order Amish are mended antiques or copies of pre-World War II models. Keeping them functioning requires careful maintenance. The Amishmen who run machine shops for repairs are kept very busy.

Water flows by gravity from tanks where it is stored after being harnessed from a well by a windmill or from a stream by a waterwheel. On some farms the same 12 hp diesel engine that powers the milking machine and the cooler operates a water pump. A diesel is also necessary to recharge batteries, another chore in Amish country. Batteries that run the flashers and turn signals for night buggy travel require frequent recharging.

For the Amish, bigger is not better, unless it's a grape the size of a plum that was God's doing. Operating a self-sufficient farm by family cooperation and without government aid is a way of integrity.

Growing Up

A lot of living has gone on in Jake Zook's brick farmhouse. Four generations have been born on the same property. His grandfather built the stucco extension or *grosdaddihaus* when his parents married.His mother was born in the back bedroom and so were all her children. The doctor got there for all the births but one. The creek was flooded and the road closed so her husband Abner delivered the second boy. Jake's the youngest so he lives on the family farm.

His wife Rebecca had her fifth child this winter. With a wide part in the middle caused by rolling her hair tightly, she looks older than her twenty-six years, but her contented face makes up for the aging. It was at Annie's quilting that she told me that she just got all her scrapple in the pans before the baby came. "I'm one to work up to the very last minute."

An Amish family welcomes a newborn with warmth but little fanfare. There are no ceremonies to mark the occasion. No baby showers. No religious dedications. If the baby is born at home as preferred, the husband leaves his farm work to contact the midwife or doctor and direct the household. In Rebecca's case, her niece came to help with the housework and, *Grossmommy* as grandma is called in their dialect, came from next door to take care of the newborn and little ones.

The Amish view children as a gift from the Lord and frown on contraception. One woman told me that she wouldn't use anything to prevent birth. But another cautiously informed a non-Amish friend that she uses the natural methods promoted by a local Catholic hospital.

From babyhood children go wherever the family goes; wear Amish clothes and learn to speak the Pennsylvania German dialect. This linguistical boundary builds a strong Amish identity. A woman wearing toeless heels talked to a very small girl in Dutch. Soon the girl tugged at her mother's apron and asked in her dialect, "Why does the woman speak Amish and have English shoes on?" "English" refers to people of the larger society who are not "dressed plain."

A parent commonly explains an action to a questioning four-year-old with, "This is *unserer weg* (our way). Lydiann was waiting with her mother on the porch of an non-Amish neighbor. "What is that?" she pointed to a decorative electric lamp.

"It makes light," her mother answered.

"Why don't we have one?"

"It's not Amish," was the answer. That was reason enough.

Preschoolers learn to show respect for authority. Grownups expect a child to obey and include the young ones in family activities, meals and group work such as pea-shelling.

A child takes responsibility in the family early. A five-year-old takes a container of milk down the road to a neighbor by foot or steers a wagon. Elementary children may drive a pony and cart along a rural road to do a family errand. Skill in handling a team develops over the years, starting with hitching up their playmates.

The patterns of Amish life and the work habits that support them imprint each child. Growing up Amish is very important to being one. One teen said, "You almost have to be born Amish to work like we do." Amish children gain a sense of belonging from working hard. They feel needed.

"I need the children's help," said one mother of seven, "and they are happy helping, with a few complaints once in a while. They are glad for a day off, but often they run out of things to do."

School Days

The teacher Leah Glick pulled the bell rope to announce the end of recess. I wondered if my greatgrandfather had heard the same bell when he attended this one-room Amish-Mennonite school in the 1880s.

Outside, the children left their softball game, got a quick drink at the hand pump and hung their jackets on hooks in the anteroom. Then Miss Glick set the timer on her desk. In three minutes it rang, and all 36 "scholars" (as the Amish call their students) from first through eighth grade scrambled into wooden schooldesks.

The room had necessities: a woodstove with a teakettle to heat water for washing hands in a basin before lunch; a peg for each drinking cup; and rods above the stove with clothespins attached to dry gloves in the winter. The alphabet and numbers marched along the wall above the blackboard; a clock in the front said 8:30 a.m. and would tick away the school day which ended at 3:30 p.m.

The children were attentive. "We will now begin a geography lesson," teacher Glick said softly. Grades 2-8 took out their books and began reading the assignment written on a bookmark. "First graders, please go to the blackboard. We are going to write letters and numbers." Leah, dressed in plain clothes and white prayer head covering, gave directions, "Make a 2." If the children did not follow, she distinctly repeated the instruction, aware that these young ones were learning the English language. "The other way, Solly. Yours is turned the wrong way."

Like most teachers at Amish schools, Leah finished eighth grade and was tapped to teach because of qualities observed while she was a "scholar". Her skills come from intuition and experience.

Students in the other grades who do not know how to pronounce a word put up a hand. In her long skirt and black, soft-soled shoes Leah moves quickly up the aisles and whispers the word being pointed to. Soon she asks the first graders to return to their seats and color a picture.

Second graders go to the front of the room and stand on a straight line on the floor, ready to answer questions about their reading. The lesson told how a boy their age was going to the grocery store to buy some fresh peas. The store in the text was different from a supermarket in that the boy received personal service just like in a small town in the fifties when this book was published. The textbooks used here were offered by a public school that was adopting a new series.

School supplies, fuel and salaries come out of the fees collected by the directors from each pupil's family. Older folks also donate. Amish pay these fees in addition to taxes that finance the public schools that they do not use. Each grade works through two readers a year plus books in arithmetic, health, science, history and geography.

During recitation Leah used game techniques such as "trapping" and "two by two" to keep the students interested. She encouraged accuracy, patiently helping each student. When one child repeatedly could not answer, the teacher reminded him that he usually understands what he reads. She did not compare him unfavorably or rebuke him but quietly encouraged him.

Each morning a section of the Bible is read. The children make pictures and print the week's Bible verse on them. Horses are a favorite illustration. I could hear them occasionally trotting past the school windows on the nearby road.

For Amish "scholars," telling time, doing practical math problems and writing legibly are important. Their families depend on written communiques either brought by friends or sent in the mail because they have no phones.

After all lessons were finished and workbooks and drawings collected, the children did their classroom chores and got their wraps by rows. I noticed a glow in the eyes of one nine-year-old. It was the first day she was wearing a belted apron. Before her birthday she wore a pinafore, the dress of the little ones.

"Goodbye, teacher", the students said cheerily as they left the room past the motto on the bulletin board: "Happiness is found along the way, not at the end of the road". For outdoor people it was long enough at the desk and they were eager to skate, walk or scooter home. Some of the Mennonite children biked.

I imagined that my great grandfather's school day resembled this one.

Maybe he tagged the same oak tree when he played hide and seek. A few of the windows had an uneven glaze and no doubt had escaped being broken by a foul ball for almost a century.

Leah Glick shyly offered to share with me the daily record of her teaching experiences. "You must remember," she warned, "that the negative feelings often went away by the next morning." Her diary entries show how she gives attention to the varied aspects of life for children ranging from 6 to 13 years. These edited excerpts also point out how closely the church community is connected to the school program.

Aug. 31. First day of school. There are 29 pupils; 4 more will move here late in the fall. Aaron tried my patience already. I just hope I can win him. I felt the strength of God by my side. I hope I can have faith in Him so that I can be a Christian example to these many watchful eyes.

I dismissed at dinnertime. The day was over much too soon.

Sept. 2. One student was chewing gum during school hours. He had to stand up front and stick it on his nose.

We had our first visitor: a little yellow kitten.

Sept. 7. Second grade had the arithmetic problem 9+2. Elam said he has 9 fingers and only one more, not two.

I can't see why flies get more attention than a teacher.

Oct. 11. It was pretty cold this morning. I did not bother to start a fire as I thought it might warm up soon, but we were almost frozen till dinnertime. We played prisoners' base (an outdoor running game) to get warm.

It was too noisy when we made leaves with acorn faces in art.

Nov. 14. Some pupils are trying hard to learn their poem while the others are learning how hard their poem is!

We dismissed at 12:00 because I wanted to go to my great aunt Rebecca's funeral.

I'm glad I cleaned the windows yesterday. David Zook wants to put the storm windows up.

Dec. 15. Many excuse cards are coming back. Some reasons (for absenteeism) are "sickly"; "sore throat"; "funeral" and "His stomach was out of shape". Being brought up as a Pennsylvania Dutch girl, I know what that meant!

The pupils are all excited about Christmas. Today we made 15 fruit baskets for the neighbors. We put a can of juice in the middle and then two of six different fruits plus cookies and candy. They sure looked nice tied up with a bow. The 5th through 8th graders delivered them.

They had a hi-ho time.

Jan. 8. David forgot his boots again! I guess I must train them to walk after him wherever he goes!

It's after school. Sam is sitting in the chair beside my desk to get his work done. If I stand by him, he finishes in a jiffy, but ... .

The girls had a good attitude toward their work today. Our visitor today was Rachel Lapp (David B's).

Jan. 14. The fields are covered with snow plus a good sheet of ice on top. During play period the pupils were sledding on Sam Stoltzfus' field. They couldn't stop talking about the wonderful sliding.

The 5th to 8th graders are making rugs from strips I brought along. Harold says that his is only big enough for his foot after four days. Happy rugging!

Feb. 24. At dinnertime we saw a great flock of snow geese fly overhead. Is spring just around the corner?

Tonight I heard a rumor that my schoolhouse burned down. All of a sudden my old, old school became of great value. This building has had so many years of scrapes and scratches. As I was sweeping I thought how long the grooves have been swept. I'm afraid a new one could never replace this love-bound school. We must remember that there is a Higher Hand who can help us in time of trouble.

March 16. After geography we cleaned our classroom. We were trying to kill the germs. So many are out with the mumps. John said he's going to Elam's place to get them! Good luck! Everyone helped clean so willingly. The pupils can sure make a teacher proud of them!

Today our visitors were Mary Burkholder and Daniel King. It was good to see them because visitors are scarce these days. Daniel said, "Keep up the good work!"

I have the tests ready for duplication. I know how the children feel about taking them even though we have worked getting ready for them.

March 24. Today Mary Stoltzfus and I visited .... School. They do many things the same, but there was no prayer at dinnertime. The scholars could sing so well. To dismiss the children, she called their parents' name. It would be nice to have just four grades but I wouldn't know which four I would want.

It was raining hard, and the horse was uncooperative.

April 4. The day was unforgettable. There were so many hands waving with questions during phonics. Some couldn't do their arithmetic; it just wouldn't sink in. I also had to remind my standing-up John to sit down; find my disappearing Amos B.; keep Minnie at her work; look at a loose tooth; bandage a bruise; hunt a lost paper besides keeping the stove from getting too hot and trying to keep patient and cool.

May 6. Our pet show was interesting. There were guinea pigs, dogs, kittens, two ducklings and a little bird without feathers. Ugh, what a smell! Titus came with some ants, his "only true lovable pet and his mother's enemy". Some of the pupils brought a younger brother or sister as their pet.

May 8. No one cried about the tests this year. I believe they sort of enjoyed them. They are all wondering if they passed. I said, "Wait and see." One boy said, "That is what my Daddy says."

At the Board meeting the parents were too busy to come and play baseball against the pupils for our end-of-school picnic. Oh, well, they can get more of their work done and we'll eat the ice cream by ourselves. Parents were very cooperative this year and that affects teaching.

May 10. A cloudy day - the last day. When I was alone in the schoolhouse each child silently slipped through my mind, each finding a special place in my heart.

Amish Vocational School

Malinda King and I were dishing up dinner, the noon meal. Steaming yams were piled high, and the lima beans that we had just shelled were swimming in buttery milk. I heard carriage wheels on the gravel driveway. "That's Naomi coming from vocational school; she's fourteen," Malinda explained, serving beef chunks and gravy that she had brought from the cellar where wooden shelves held dozens of home-canned jars of food for winter use. "When our children finish eighth grade, they attend school each week for three hours and keep a journal of the homemaking and farm work they do the rest of the time. The government allows us to do this until they're fifteen rather than send them to public high school."

While we enjoyed a meal that had been in the garden at breakfast, Naomi said at school she had worked on arithmetic problems and studied German. This language study will help her to read and understand the Bible and songs at church.

Malinda was passing milk to pour on cake and fresh peaches for dessert. "Those few hours a week don't seem like very much, but we're real careful to keep them because we want to safeguard this opportunity. She was quiet as though she wasn't sure if she

should continue. "My father went to prison in the fifties rather than send my brother to high school. I was twelve then, and I remember feeling cautious of outsiders." Amish refusal to attend consolidated schools gave rise to both public ire and sympathy and eventually a case filed on behalf of the Amish.

A 1972 Supreme Court decision exempted the Amish from attending high school. Chief Justice Warren Burger wrote: "Amish objection to formal education beyond the eighth grade is firmly grounded in central religious beliefs. They object to the high school and higher education generally because the values it teaches are in marked variance with Amish values and the Amish way of life. The high school tends to emphasize intellectual and scientific accomplishments, self-distinction, competitiveness, worldly success and social life with other students. Amish society emphasizes informal learning-through-doing, a life of 'goodness,' rather than a life of intellect; wisdom, rather than technical knowledge; community welfare, rather than competition; and separation, rather than integration with contemporary world society."

Youth and Marriage

"I counted the days and nights and then hours until I would be sixteen," remembered 18-year-old Dan Kauffman. A landmark age. Immediately after that birthday Amish youth begin "running around," which means joining a group or "supper gang". This group of 150-200 older teens meets Sundays to play games and sing. Driving his own horse and buggy, a boy may take his sister as far as 20 miles - a 21/2 hour ride - to the home where a family has invited the gang for afternoon volleyball or softball. Only the boys play, while the girls chatter and admire from the sidelines and then serve a treat of perhaps lemonade and pretzels.

Sarah Beiler told me she and her sister fixed twenty pizzas when her group, The Sparkies, met at their farm. A young person may choose any group. Sarah attended one group three Sundays before six girls her age decided together to join the Souvenirs, a smaller group. She admitted that each group has a character and may have a reputation for being "plainer" or "faster". Parents' training influences the group a girl or boy runs around with.

Amish society derives strength from age group associations. All the girls who turn 16 in one year become a "buddy bunch". These girls often become close friends, eventually attending each others' weddings. If the percentage of newcomers greatly increases in any year, the group may split to maintain a balance between the new "buddy bunch" and the older teens. The host gets plenty of help with the 4 p.m. milking. Often the "gang" moves back to the home where church was held that morning to spend several hours singing. The tempo is livelier for the choruses than ancient hymns, but the words are usually in German.

Dating is allowed at age 16, but many Amish youth spend two or more years socializing with the "gang" before a boy singles out a specific girl. The singings offer a venue for learning to know something about potential marriage partners.

The guy takes his mate home from singings and spends other Sunday evenings at her home. Some girls are going steady by 16; some marry past 20. A dating couple may visit a married sister and play games such as Flinch and Sorry. Playing face cards is taboo. Curfews are not an issue; a young man may be unharnessing his horse near dawn.

A teen said, "You must remember that we're human first, and then we're Amish." Some married couples privately see the bishop to confess courtship intimacies. For six weeks they may be "excommunicated for their young days". After some instruction, they again become "church members in good standing".

Amish usually do not become baptized church members until they are about to marry. Parents and church elders accept that the teens are a time for "tasting the world". Some young men may secretly buy cars or try drinking. Sarah offered her assessment, "Our young people drink to be smart, to be big. It's a sinful thing, an Amish weakness." Occasional accidents result from their inexperienced and perhaps unlicensed driving. When I asked if they were modelling adults, she said, "I have never seen an adult drink socially. Some of my relatives make dandelion or berry wine for medicinal purposes."

Other young men stretch the boundaries by "shingling" or layering their hair or "destroying the Amish look" in other ways. A youth who sports a Hawaiian print shirt will not be too surprised if his mother silently turns it into a tea towel.

A young woman may also bend the rules. On a Sunday morning walk I saw a girl in Amish garb riding in a car duck to avoid recognition. The church frowns on the heart-shaped head prayer coverings that young girls prefer. In one family a girl may exercise her adolescent independence by making her bedroom "real fancy" with candles, artificial flowers and dishes. Sarah explained that her parents understood that she "wanted things that were allowed but not necessary. On shopping trips, they sometimes gave me money for such things."

She was wearing the usual plain work dress and gray apron, but from a side profile it was obvious that Sarah was pregnant. And she was eager to share her views on child-rearing. "Training determines the respect children have for authority. I hope my child wants to obey instead of my saying, 'You must.' If an Amish young person goes one step, then the next one away from the right comes easily. Often that first step is keeping some of the money they earn rather than giving all to their parents. That usually means they want to buy something that they want to hide.

"It's good for our young people to repent before the

church - even if people don't know your wrong. Hiding it affects the whole community."

We were sitting in Sarah's big, wide kitchen. The clock above the sink and long L of wooden cupboards had hands that moved around a painted ceramic plate. Measuring cups, a mug tree, and a match holder stood on her long counter. A new rolltop desk and a sofa for a noontime snooze were most likely used by her husband. In the future sick or playful children will rest there.

She and Reuben were married last wedding season, but the home her parents remodelled for them was large enough to accommodate the seven children of a typical Old Order family. While we talked, she handstitched and stuffed a calico hanging that tourists will buy in her friend's gift shop. The pendulum of the large grandfather's clock made by her father reflected on the shiny printed linoleum. Another hand-crafted functional piece was the padded sewing machine stool with oak drawers for storage and rollers for easy moving. This was a sweetheart present from Reuben.

From Sarah and other friends I learned the high points of the wedding of David Zook and Barbara Stoltzfus. Other Old Order weddings are similar.

November is wedding month among the Amish in Lancaster County. After fall communion at church, a young couple's wedding date is "published" or announced during Sunday morning preaching. No wonder David and Barbara were not present. What was rumored is true! These steady beaus will be married three Thursdays from now at 9 a.m. Where? At Barbara's parents' home, of course.

What bustle and preparations! In Amish communities, a wedding day is a feast day. The house must shine as well as the dishes that will serve two full meals. There are personal invitations to deliver locally and postcards to mail to relatives far away.

Guests arrive in their carefully brushed black suits and Sunday dresses. Their horses are put to meadow for a day of grazing while they hand over a fancy dessert to the uncle at the doorway. Inside, guests sit on backless benches set in rows facing where the minister will stand.

An Amish wedding begins with music, one singer starting a song that resembles a Gregorian chant with the others joining with strength. Each German word may bear several notes, each one slow and measured. Their voices are unaccompanied.

Near the end of an hour of singing, the ministers, David and Barbara, and their four attendants, came from upstairs where the order of the service was planned and admonitions were given to the bride and groom.

During the second and main sermon Barbara and David stood before the bishop for their marriage vows. The Biblical example was taken from the book of Tobi in the Apocrypha. After this the ceremony helpers left, very quietly, to continue fixing food; but the three-hour service continued. Several men gave testimony to the sermon; then the group sang more songs.

The service over, some visited outside, but many others quietly went about their assigned tasks. Sadie and Jonas Lapp peeled and mashed potatoes; Ben Beiler and John Zook washed dishes at a dishpan for four table settings, a total of 350 people.

Amish wedding fare is prescribed and so delicious! Whole chickens were roasted and then small pieces of the meat mixed into mounds of flavorful stuffing. Mashed potatoes with gravy. Cole slaw. Celery cooked in a delicate, sweet-sour sauce. Butter, bread and jam; all homemade. Dessert features apple pie with whipped cream, a berry sauce, cookies, cream-filled doughnuts, canned peaches and coffee. Silent grace begins and ends each meal. The men sit on one side of the table and the women on the other.

The rest of the day's activities ritualize companionship and food. A long L-shaped table is set with lovely china and finger foods; cookies, apples and doughnuts. But the most outstanding one is crisp celery blanched to a yellow-green sweetness, the stalks tall in decorative glassware. A family with extra celery in the garden and a marriageable daughter is bound to be teased about a wedding!

Upstairs the unmarried girls in their late teens looked over some presents displayed in Barbara's room. (Most people in the neighborhood would give their present when the newlyweds visited them during the winter.)

Soon the wedding party came downstairs, each couple holding hands. The girls were now wearing white prayer coverings instead of the black they had on during the service. David and Barbara sat at the angle of the table with their attendants on either side.

The next event both excited and worried the young, unmarried women. As is customary, the single men went upstairs, each bringing a girl down to the L-shaped table. The friends and cousins of the groom had first choice with younger boys selecting last and often with embarrassment.

One young woman recollected, "Waiting upstairs is a terrible time for the girls. Your hands get sweaty, wondering if you're going to get picked. But once you're at the table, it's fun."

German songbooks were passed around the full table, and there were several hours of singing interspersed with talking and giggling. The adults sitting in the background joined in or carried on their own conversations. Occasionally, young marrieds brought in "gifts for the corner" - fancy cakes, iced cupcakes, ham and cheese platters, decorative candies. The bride passed these foods around the table.

In spite of the continuous munching, a hot meal was prepared for supper. Some left to milk their cows, but the singing went on past nine o'clock. There was some shifting of couples too. For instance, David's brother's girlfriend Sue was at another wedding. Today he was paired with Sally Petersheim, but later he met Sue.

The practice of pairing young people for singing sometimes results in a match for life! In spite of a very wide and close community, once in a while an unknown eligible turns up to the surprise an Amish single. Barbara's sister Sadie met her present husband at a wedding that she almost left early!

David and Barbara each went home with their own families. Though married they would spend only weekends together through the winter until all the preparations were made at their new home. In the spring they would begin housekeeping on their own.

Living arrangements vary, but they take into consideration closeness to family and the community. It would be unthinkable to move to a town or county where no Amish live. Pioneer settlements are communal decisions. Each married couple must make adjustments, but they can hold onto the familiar to do so. One woman remembers, "When we got married, I stayed in the home I was born, and my family moved to a smaller house. I was the oldest of five girls, and I missed all the bustle and laughter. I could hardly go upstairs where we girls had had our rooms. It was good that I could often be with them; they were just down the lane!"

Faith and History

During the Reformation in Europe Martin Luther and Ulrich Zwingli upturned pietistic practices in the Catholic Church. A third group of reformers known as the Anabaptists were more radical, believing baptism was for adults who stated their faith. They also promoted a separation of church and state. The latter issue, in particular, brought these "rebaptizers" persecution. They became known as Mennonites because Menno Simons, a former Catholic priest from Holland, was one of their leaders.

It was not until 150 years later that the Amish evolved as a split from the Mennonite Anabaptists. The Amish get their name from their headstrong founder, Jacob Amman, who felt that the Mennonite Church in the late seventeenth century was too casual about church discipline. With determination, he promoted several practices, the main one being social avoidance of people who were expelled from the church. Such shunning known as *Meidung* means not traveling, doing business or eating with a former church member. The practice stems from I Corinthians 5:11 in the Bible: "But now I have written unto you not to keep company, if any man that is called a brother be a fornicator, or covetous, or an idolater, or a railer or a drunkard, or an extortioner; with such an one not to eat." Amman's followers of this strict practice became known as the Amish.

Today Amish shun in varying degrees. Many softpedal Meidung, allowing their sense of Biblical forgiveness to overrule. At weddings or funerals, family members who have left the Old Order Amish for a more liberal church may be seated at a different table with only a crack of space separating the two tables. They told me of their care not to embarrass friends and family members by relating to them inappropriately.

A mid-age woman explained her experience. "I grew up Old Order, the group also called "home Amish" because they have church in their homes. My mother was very hurt when my husband and I left and joined the "church Amish" (thus called because they have a church building). It's some years now, and although she'll ride with me a long distance, she follows the ban, as it is called, in the neighborhood because others expect her to."

Naomi Smucker told me that her father's shunning ranged from ridiculous to excruciating for her as the victim. "He would ride with me in my car, but I couldn't drive. And when he was on his deathbed, I could fix his food, but I couldn't feed it to him. "

Amish ways are determined by their interpretation of the Bible and the *Ordnung,* the unwritten rules of a church district. The standards of dress, home decorating, transportation and farm practice are known by all members; many practices have held for generations. Borderline matters are often discussed at a semi-annual meeting of ministers and bishops. It is important that agreement and peace abide in the community before the members have communion each spring and fall. At this Sunday service, those who have been baptized and are in "good standing" (anyone who has erred may confess and be forgiven) take a bit of bread broken off of a slice cut from a homemade loaf and a swallow of wine.

Later members wash each other's feet to symbolize loving service towards each other. Jacob Amman felt foot-washing was very important, and the practice emerged also in the Mennonite Church after settlement in the United States.

Lifestyle standards are determined by one's group or church district. The 20-35 households in each are geographically close enough to travel to each others' homes for Sunday morning preaching. Church is held every other week; families spend other Sundays resting and visiting. They do only essential work such as milking the cows; they do not buy or sell. Roadside stands at Amish homes wear signs, "No Sunday Sales".

There are many preparations for a family having church. Besides cleaning the house and trimming the yard, they must open the sliding or folding doors between rooms to make one open area. An enclosed horse-drawn cart transports backless benches set up in rows for the service.

The week before the Glicks were having church, Anna Mary invited me to help her get ready. She was doing her housecleaning, a major once-over that the Amish housewife expects to do each spring and fall. We wiped the shiny green walls in the kitchen and also the brown woodwork and cupboards grained with a feather.

Anna Mary's pace was steady but determined. As she tackled dirt that naturally accumulated from a family of seven, she watched the jars of grapes boiling in a canner on the stove and also listened for any horn tooting from the vegetable stand down their short lane. And all the while she was telling me about the "preaching service", as the Amish call their bi-weekly worship.

"We sing at least two songs until the ministers come down the stairs. One of them gives the *Anfang* "the short" sermon, about a half hour. He speaks in Pennsylvania Dutch, quoting Scripture in High German. There is silent prayer and then comments and a chapter in the Bible read by the deacon. We use the Luther translation of the Bible.

"The main sermon is an hour of Biblical interpretation. The same minister then reads a prayer from *Christenpflicht.*, which means A Christian's Duty. We often hear the phrase, 'holding on to...' because if we follow our traditions, which are based on the Bible, we will not be led astray."

Amish feel that the fellowship meal held afterwards strengthens relationships. Abram King, a white-bearded great grandfather told me that it often takes 15 minutes to shake hands goodbye. But food comes first.

Anna Mary continues, "Each host family serves the same menu so there's no competition. The girls and I will make 30 *snitz* pies Saturday morning; they're filled with dried apples."

When I exclaimed over such a baking, Anna Mary assured me that that wasn't very many pies, that some families had to bake 50, and that they would surely be finished by 10 a.m. since the oven was large. I didn't dare mention that my own crusts come from the supermarket; I knew that these would originate from the 100-pound bag of flour in the pantry.

Other foods, usually cold, are bologna, pickled red beets, and homemade cup cheese, and are served with coffee. "Several families will bring homemade bread, and I will mix up a spread of molasses and peanut butter," Anna Mary described. "We put out only cups, saucers and knives so the dishes are few."

There are two tables, one for the men and another for the women. The older folks eat first with tables filled and refilled until everyone has been served. I wondered if there were any crumbs for the church mice!

Being together must be more precious for people who do not assume they can communicate by phone. There is much to exchange. People tend to socialize within their peer group, but the young also observe the older ones who greet and perhaps softly tease their juniors. It's a time to plan a "sisters' day", when the women meet at one of their homes to quilt or do other work. The men talk about crop news, which farms had hail damage to their tobacco or how early the corn is maturing this year. The schoolteacher may ask the supervisor in charge of maintenance to check on the malfunctioning coal stove. And news from other Amish settlements is shared.

Just now in Anna Mary's kitchen I was enjoying the home setting without dozens of people. The scent of drying tobacco wafted from the open shed, mingling with the pungent aroma of grapes. Outside, the men were talking to their horses and each other as they hauled in another load of corn stalks for the silo. The clock on the shelf chimed, and I accepted its melodic interruption as a symbol of the harmony of this home's sounds. No phone jangled; no dishwasher hissed; no TV or radio blared. There was silence for being and thinking.

Back to work. I climbed a ladder to wipe the top of a tall cabinet. Inside the glass doors were books with German words on the spines. There were several *Ausbunds*, the main hymnal of the Amish and the oldest Protestant songbook still in publication. One of its praise hymns included since the 1622 edition is always the second song at an Amish church service.

Anna Mary saw me looking at the larger books. "When Chris and I got married, my parents gave us a family Bible; a New Testament prayer book; an *Ausbund* and a Martyr's Mirror. This latter book documents the persecution of our people and other Anabaptists in Europe."

Now the windows were sparkling, and the green shades free of fly dirt. Such a plain window dressing, with no curtains to press or drapes to dryclean, certainly simplified cleaning. Only two chores remained; sweeping the wooden floors and shaking the carpets. Four woven runners, one-yard wide, covered the parlour floor. Brighter throw rugs dressed up the typical blue-gray carpets.

Earlier on a hot summer night I had found Anna Mary and her daughters cutting up old clothes and tying the strips into bundles. "We'll take these to an Amishman who weaves them on a loom."

Amish rag carpets, made of cotton warp with worn-out clothing woven in, last half a century. Enough lengths to cover a floor may cost $175, a single-lifetime purchase. There are several Amish craftsmen who provide this service from home shops. One in Lancaster County works at his loom in the winter and makes brooms from corn straw in the summer.

Useful Beauty

As a child, I liked the scent of our quilts fresh off the washline but envied the soft-tufted chenille spreads on my friends' beds. Quilting was an assumed part of my tradition that my Mennonite grandmas didn't want lost on this "town girl". I well remember the day my paternal grandmother adjusted the black strings on her prayer covering and bent down to me. "Well, Ruth, you're in school now; you'll want to learn your hand sewing."

I wasn't too surprised when I opened my Christmas present that year and saw a sewing basket filled with neat stacks of squares to make my first four-patch quilt. Grandpa had cut them from scraps from my dresses. They looked more like an assignment than a gift. But my grandmother's praise at how my first corners met precisely in the middle were so lavish that I took on the challenge of sewing enough patches by hand to master the skill. To this day I prefer hand stitching to using a machine.

It's not always been so with the Amish. Ever since they adopted quilting from their "English" neighbors in the nineteenth century, they have pieced their patchwork on treadle sewing machines. Beforehand, with cardboard patterns, they cut out bars, squares, diamonds, rectangles, triangles and petals from material scraps and sewed them into a pleasing design for the quilt top. Certain patterns became standard, but each maker varies the colors and the border to make her own unique bedcover.

Next, a filling (in the past wool batting and today a synthetic) is added for warmth and heaviness. The backing, once flannel or cotton printed material, may be pieced or a wide stretch of plain fabric. All three layers are fastened into a wooden quilting frame.

Quilting stitches often follow the route of the piecework. For example, the quilting on a Lone Star pattern goes one-quarter inch inside the diamonds that make up the huge star. Templates of cardboard or plastic are used to mark the quilting pattern in open areas.

I asked for a bit of Lydia Esh's time because she is an Old Order woman who is a discriminating judge of quilt quality and markets them. She was canning applesauce the day I stopped by so I pared some apples while I listened. "The artistic quality of a quilt is determined by the colors; how the corners of the piecework meet and whether the quilting is even." She said a quilt lasts for decades, with the fabric wearing out before the quilting comes out. "The quilts my mother got from home were still used on our beds when I left home.

"Many of the quilt preferences of Amish are also top sellers among other people. We like to use feathers, both rings and swirls, as quilting designs. Hearts are also popular.

"Many Amish girls don't get interested in quilting until they're 18. By then, their mothers are putting in quilts for the children to take when they marry. A daughter may get as many as five; a son a few less." Lydia's preschooler Jonathan was begging in Dutch to turn the handle of the saucemaker. She allowed him, and after a few tries, he was content and started hauling blocks in his trucks.

"Now, where were we?" Lydia asked as she put another kettle of apple halves on the stove.

I wondered which fabrics are preferred. "Today we Amish use calico prints and other fabrics that we buy. We might ask a clerk to help us match the colors. Years ago, we used only the colors that we wear." We both knew that the antique quilts of Amish magenta, purple, lavender, forest green and robin egg blue with very close quilting are collectors' items.

She continued, "There are some very popular patterns. Dahlia, for instance, is liked by us and is also a bestseller. My daughter has a pink one on her bed, and I put a blue one in the boys' room. Boys don't really care what's on their beds. We often use dark colors for them."

A woman's main task is to shelter, feed and clothe her family. For a husband and eight children, this is a full-time job for thirty-eight year old Naomi Lapp. While she was shelling limas out of her apron, she informed me that even if she sewed an article of clothing every day of the year, each member would have a sparse wardrobe. She tackles under and outerwear, sets of dress clothes and work garments, even making the bands on her sons' straw hats out of black ribbon.

Family garments must meet church standards of plainness. Naomi sews black broadfall pants and colored shirts for the men and boys. Their Sunday garb is a white shirt, black vest and, in cool weather, a straight coat without lapels that fastens with hooks and eyes. For herself and her daughters, a woman sews dresses with a scooped neckline and a long skirt with pleats in the back. Solid-colored fabrics of royal, robin, or turquoise blue; deep purple or magenta and dark green or brown are favorites. Gray, black and white aprons are sewn to straight-pin onto the front of the dress, the color determined by age and occasion. She teaches her daughters to sew all these items as well as the white organdy prayer coverings worn over their hair twisted into a bun.

Besides clothing, she enjoys creating other decorative necessities with the scraps, discards and remnants. She may wrap tin cans with cloth; stitch them together and cover the whole to make a hassock. She embroiders pillowcases and crochets a lace edging around them. She pieces cushion tops for the rocker; hooks throw rugs and makes hot mats for kitchen use. A woman feels satisfaction to turn useless scraps into items that give her family warmth and comfort and her home beauty and color.

For her husband the sweaty toil of fieldwork creates a landscape productive and beautiful. His strip farming makes patterns across the fields that are their own artwork.

His wife feels similarly about her garden. With expert management, she plans her preserving according to the harvest. While she focuses on getting the produce prepared for the jars or the locker before it spoils, she delights in the size and amount of the vegetables and their eye-pleasing rows.

The edge row of the garden is usually flowers with additional beds in the yard, under trees or beside the milkhouse. Reds and yellows stand brilliant against green foliage. Yardwork is for females, and many women and girls not only weed but also slice the turf edge even with a knife.

From Seed to Harvest

The average Amish farm here is 55 acres, much smaller than most tractor-operated farms in America. The Amish farm size has declined over the twentieth century because the soaring land prices forced farmers to subdivide for their offspring. "We also learned that with crop rotation, stripping and hybrid seed we could produce as much on 50 acres as my grandfather did on 100," explained Joe Esh, a retired farmer who still works on his sons' land. "The bottom line for us is handling acreage that a family can work and live by. My one son's family of eight farms and markets seven acres of fruits and vegetables. The younger one with five children milks 30 cows on 60 acres of land. They both make a living."

A farmer puts about 60 per cent of his tillable soil in grains. Corn is high-energy, as work for the farmer and as fodder for the livestock. The corn and alfalfa or other hays such as clover or timothy feed and bed the farm's 30-40 dairy cows and also maintain the horses and mules that the family keeps for draught and road power. Six or so acres of wheat may become part of a dry ration for the animals or may be sold. Another cash crop is tobacco, so labor-intensive that a family with 6-8 children seldom plants more than five acres.

Such diversification requires careful organization. An Amish farmer becomes a master at timing, meeting the needs of each crop and land strip as well as keeping his horses sound and his equipment maintained.

There is work for all seasons. A farmer paces his work, maximizing each season by spending long hours behind his mules and horses. It takes us longer to do field work so we begin earlier," explained one farmer.

"This is a privilege, to care for the earth God created." Amish farmers act on the mandate "to keep and dress it" in Genesis of the Old Testament.

The winter spreading of manure and lime is followed by turning over the soil; ploughing, harrowing and rolling until the earth is smooth and even. Alfalfa is a preferred hay in Lancaster County because at maturity one growing season may yield four cuttings. It is planted early April with wheat and seed corn going into the ground by May. A two-horse cultivator keeps the young plants weed-free.

At the same time a farmer raising potatoes must cultivate and spray them several times. Joe remembers his sprayer disturbing hundreds of moths as he went up each row. Their ascent attracted martin birds that pursued him, gobbling the moths in flight.

Turning and baling the first cutting of alfalfa goes on in June. Other grains or grasses such as oats, barley or timothy will be ready to harvest this month with wheat ripe and golden in July. Farmers work cooperatively to haul the picturesque shocks to the barn for threshing and then baling the straw. The basic principle is "I'll help do yours and you can pitch in on my crop."

There is a brief respite mid-summer that may enable families to work at building projects or hire a van to visit distant relatives.

Getting in corn, tobacco and another crop of alfalfa

fills September and October with long field days. A farmer chops a third of his corn acreage into silage and lets the rest dry for shell and ear corn. To harvest green corn, a team of 4-6 mules pulls a cutter that hoists the stalks onto a wagon. This is pulled to the base of a silo where an insulage cutter run by a stationary engine chops the roughage. A hydraulic elevator or fan fills the silo.

Weeks later, after the remaining stalks are brown, a mule-drawn corn picker plucks off the ears, and an auxiliary motor, acceptable as long as it doesn't touch the soil, shoots them into a wagon pulled by another team. With his younger children in school, a father is grateful for the help of a teen son at corn harvest. Its completion signals the end of gathering and the beginning of the wedding season, a time for feasting.

Labor-intensive tobacco requires long hours and strong arms from the whole family. Efforts to mechanize the process have failed, so Amish today raise tobacco in much the same way their parents did. In spring the head of the household buys tobacco plants raised in a sterilized seedbed. May is the time to transplant these seedlings into well-spaced rows. Two people ride a horse-drawn transplanter, dropping the plants into a row. The machine waters and covers the roots.

Hoeing tobacco is one of a child's earliest field tasks. A horse-drawn cultivator helps keep the weeds cleared. As the rich green leaves lengthen, they receive meticulous care; spraying, fertilizing and topping. Pinching off the suckers to prevent flowering makes a strong thumb. When the leaves are mature in September, whole families take to the fields to cut the stalks with a shears and spear them onto 48-inch lathes to hang on a specially-built wagon frame. Lifting a full lathe weighing at least 25 pounds is known as "heavy work". Throughout the fall the leaves hang in rows from floor to ceiling in the tobacco shed, drying in the sun and air flowing through the vented building.

When they are brown and cured, usually by November, the leaves are stripped from the stalk and bundled in bales for shipment. Potential buyers inspect the crop and make an offer on the basis of quality. A farmer hopes to have his tobacco check in time for the March sales when he may invest in farm machinery, livestock or land for a son if his own farm is paid off.

Attuned to the annual cycle, Amish farmers accept the balance of productive and slim years. As "stewards" of God's soil, they blend farm tasks and family responsibility, trusting the Genesis promise of "seedtime and harvest, cold and heat, summer and winter" to continue.

Family and Community

With most life events happening at home, the Amish family is the core of the community's strength. The extended family rallies to help when an accident or handicap wears on the nuclear family. Church members depend on each other before they turn to non-Amish institutions. For example, special schools serve mentally and emotionally handicapped children.

The family and community informally help each member find meaningful work. A blind Amishman makes brooms. A dwarfed woman found typing at an Amish business rewarding work. Another man, who lost his ability to walk in an accident, operates a store to earn a livelihood.

I drove down the long lane of his family's farm one late summer day when the breeze was blowing the cornflowers and goldenrod. Jonathan Beiler sat behind the counter supervising the opening day of a sale in his variety store. Beiler pushed his wheelchair to a table and explained that he had been selling since his injury. "When my parents were building this house, we learned of an Old Order couple who wanted to sell their store because of their age. We enlarged the house, and my aunt went in with me; we're co-managers. Now I'm not bored in the winter because people come here all year round." Beiler can wheel his chair between the store and his home and also down the aisles of toys, dishes, candles and rakes. Most of his customers are Amish and other plain folks.

Raising children is an honor in Amish life, but some women do not marry. One 31-year-old single wrote in Family Life, an Amish magazine: "Being the unchosen one in my circle of friends has caused me to feel inferior... Why does God who is not a respector of persons plan that the pretty girls and those from popular families will get partners while those who are not considered as 'somebody' will stay single? "

Despite such ponderings, unmarrieds often fill a valued place in the Amish community. Some teach school; others run their own enterprises. Annie Stoltzfoos explained how she made the leap from her parents' home to being on her own. "Until children are 21, they give all their earnings to their parents. When I was almost of age, I knew I had to make it on my own. I thought of baking, but you lose all your profit if you have to sell leftover goods at half price. I was glad when my brother started farming and asked me to keep house for him. But now he's getting married so I'm planning to live with my aunt and sell quilts."

Ten years ago an Amish bishop told me that in the future Amish homesteads in Lancaster County would be dotted with workshops as in Switzerland. His prediction has come true.

A high growth rate and the soaring price of farmland due to industrial expansion around them have forced Amish to look for income alternatives to farming. Also, their community in Lancaster County is now large enough to support small enterprises that can hire and serve Amish. They make carriages, clocks, batteries, silos, wagons, cabinetry, quilts and toys, and sell books, dishes, dogs, baked goods, eggs and seasonal produce.

Some selling is a sideline. For example, whenever a woman's housework slows, she can pick up needle and quilt, earning so much per yard of thread. Lydia Esh fields out work to women who cut patches, piece, quilt or bind quilts. A quilt selling for $450 may bring income to five different households. Quilts and other handicrafts sell well to non-Amish tourists and residents.

But many shops support a whole family and provide extra income for others. Two women operating a home business mentioned that when they heard that some families were needing more earnings, they decided to show others how to make their chow chow, a mixture of pickled vegetables. Why not have others help supply our markets? they asked. Personal profits were not a business priority. On the day that I joined their production team I saw and gained rewards more substantial than dollars.

The task of this July day was to finish chopping 30 bushels of red peppers that could not be sold in supermarkets because of their funny shapes. For three days seven or so friends and relatives had been chopping, embellishing their work with conversation and stories.

We were a circle of choppers busy with sharp knives. "Look at this one," laughed seventy-six-year-old Mary King. It looked like a barbell.

Mary would celebrate her next birthday with her twin sister at a quilting at her daughter's next week. Of course, there would be a cake.

There was more talk about twins because this family seems to specialize in them. Cousin Emma said, "Remember what happened when Amos and Christ were born? The doctor held the smaller one in his palm wondering if it was worth taking him to the hospital. He asked your opinion, Mary. You said, 'As long as there's life, there's hope.'"

"And just think, he's the stronger today," Mary added. "A father of six."

The story reaped no malice towards the doctor, only praise for Mary and delight in the retelling.

After several hours of working, Emma and her husband boarded their carriage and set off for home. "Pick a jar from the shelf," urged one of the owners of this cottage industry that markets to dozens of wholesalers as well as selling directly to customers. The day's work, dozens of gallons of red pepper pieces, were cooling. Later they would be added with nine other vegetables, at least some fresh, to be canned as chow chow. The effort of coming together had lightened the workload of these two business women.

Later Life

The Amish accept death as a part of life. The community absorbs the departure of a loved one as respectfully and honestly as a farmer watches the earth take in decaying stubble after each harvest. Even when a fatal farm or buggy accident shocks a family, the Amish explain, "The Lord giveth; the Lord taketh away." This kind of acceptance soothed the last days, funeral and burial of 62-year-old Jacob King.

Jacob had been in "a bad way" for some time, but last Tuesday he was "doing real poorly" so the children were called home. They all came and were able to talk to "Pop" through the evening, but before midnight he was gone. From the little phone house at the end of the lane, a convenience installed during Jacob's battle with heart disease, the oldest son John called the doctor, but he didn't come to sign the death certificate until four.

By dawn, word had gone out and 25 people were sitting quietly in the house to show concern and to help with the arrangements. When the funeral director arrived, the men of the family and church leaders were "making out papers" at the table. They had written the names of the relatives on both sides of the family, beginning with the closest and decided who would go in person to invite them. It was a large family with many still living so they had to stop with the oldest nieces and nephews.

The funeral was set for Friday at 9 a.m. slow time. (The Amish do not observe daylight saving time during the summer.) The Amish attach so much meaning to the body of a family member being "at home" that they insisted on home embalmings until Pennsylvania law required that the task be done in a licensed mortuary or morgue.

As soon as possible, the undertaker brought back the body clad in long underwear. Talking was hushed in the big kitchen; family members reminiscing. "His birthday was next week," one cousin noted. "Did you know that he spent the last two in the hospital? How good that the Lord took him before another one. So much suffering."

On Wednesday afternoon the sons, all three, dressed their father's body in a white shirt, vest and pants. John, a farmer, carefully pulled up white silk stockings, trying not to snag them with his rough hands. "This is the last thing I can do for Pop," he whispered in Dutch, tears slipping into his beard. The body was placed in a six-sided hardwood box, stained walnut, with a peaked lid, hinged partway for viewing.

All Amish funeral practices are the same, hardly varying over the past decades. The funeral is held at the home or barn of the deceased with neighbors and church members handling all the details of the service and meal. The cost is less than half of a non-Amish funeral because the materials are the simplest, and friends perform services that a funeral director usually does.

At least 300 people would be attending, most in carriages, those from a distance riding in hired vans. Henry and his wife Sally, who had managed the household and barn work for the past few days, assigned hostlers to unhitch the carriages and tie the horses. Henry can identify the horses of each family. "Here come Cousin John and his wife."

The hostlers tied matching numbers on each carriage and bridle so that hitching was orderly. Everyone remembers the funeral when someone forgot the tags so the hostlers used chalk. A thunderstorm broke near the end of the service and washed the numbers from the nylon buggies. What confusion when each man went to hitch his own horse, not knowing where it had been tied or his carriage parked.

Inside, the downstairs had been opened with the partitions removed to form one large room. The coffin was at one end, with the closest relatives sitting near it and the women of the church the farthest, near the kitchen.

A white cloth covered Jacob's face, and the audience sat silently until the family's three clocks chimed 9 o'clock, the time to begin.

Ministers removed their hats, and the rest of the men followed. One minister stood and addressed the group with Biblical messages. He alluded to "our brother", with no personal eulogies, only spiritual directives. He urged the members, sitting solemnly on benches, to be prepared for death.

After a second minister spoke for a half hour, he read a hymn. After the benediction, the undertaker removed the cloth and the Amish viewed the body, filing out the door. There were tears, but quiet ones. Grandson Dan held up his three-year-old to touch her great grandpop's face. "Give him your last aye-aye," he encouraged. She hesitated slightly because he looked different; he had no glasses. Then she obediently stroked his bearded cheek just like she used to when she sat on his knee.

By now the benches were cleared and the tables laid for the first 75 or so to eat. It is understood that "those that go along out (to the grave) will have the first opportunity to have a piece to eat," as translated from their dialect. The menu is expected: sliced, cold beef with hot gravy and mashed potatoes; cheese cut in squares; bread and a spread of molasses and peanut butter with home-canned fruit to sweeten the palate.

The pallbearers carried the coffin to the hearse, a slightly longer buggy owned by the undertaker but maintained by his Amish employee. And as the second table finished eating, the hostlers began hitching teams. In all the functional movement, there was a quiet calmness.

The funeral carriage procession moved to the cemetery with some direction from the local police or constable. After the horses were tied, the relatives again viewed Jacob. His face and gray beard softened in the sunlight. A tree overhead rustled its leaves, a seeming welcome from the earth. His sons and their children looked long, and then the eldest closed the wooden lid. The pallbearers lifted the coffin at the bottom where the manufacturer had kindly chiseled an insert for an easier grip and then used handstraps to lower it into the roughbox. There was a brief service, the tone hopeful, and then two shoveled dirt until the grave was completely closed.

Most relatives stayed until the mound was peaked and marked with two wooden sticks. Later the family placed a simple, white, rounded tombstone with Jake's name and the dates of his birth and death.

The routines of life return quickly. Tradition demands that female relatives wear black dresses in public. The time of mourning is one year for each parent, spouse, and sibling; six months for a grandparent or grandchild; three months for an aunt or uncle and six weeks for a cousin. Most Amish wear the black dress, cape and apron the required period for each death. One woman from a large family felt that she spent most of her youth wearing black. "I didn't think anything of it at the time."

Reflections

As a people, the Amish do change. Their ways withstand persecution for issues that threaten their separateness, but they bend on matters that do not tamper with family solidarity. Currently, the Amish are maintaining strength as some change from farm to cottage industry. "We're holding ninety-some per cent of our members," claimed one bishop. "But the next generation will tell. Amish don't need big money. If our young people get on the soft side and have an easy come, easy go attitude towards money..." he shook his head.

Their history demanded economic astuteness. Amish now use the financial acumen that was so essential to survival on the farm in other business affairs. Some Amish dare to reap a share of the valuable tourist market that has mushroomed in eastern Lancaster because of their presence. They may go for gain more earnestly in the future. In 1986 an Amishman first approached a bed and breakfast referral service to offer to rent his farm cabin to tourists. Amish adults refrain from having "their image graven" on a tourist's film but sell postcards of Amish at their roadside stand. "And making friends with tourists will affect our children," further laments the bishop.

Separateness from the world has been so important to the Amish that they have never felt inclined to explain themselves. It has always been more important to be upright than to be understood. Goodness is to be lived, not to be defended. In fact, communications and public relations are such foreign concepts in their domain of humbly following the right that they often withdraw from issues and events that create media focus. On one occasion an Amish requested a variance to keep a horse stabled in town, but withdrew it when the word hit the papers. It was more noble to comply than to attract attention.

Such a world view does not necessarily stamp out curiosity about the larger world. One young woman said, "I often wonder how non-Amish people meet people to marry. There are so many of them out there." She paused, "I know they wonder a lot of things about us. They ask such strange questions. Then I think about my curiosity about nuns. I hear they don't get married." Her voice rose, showing how incredulous that seemed. "I don't expect somebody without any religion at all to understand our ways."

In the past their ways have reflected integration of family, furrow and faith. But as Amish exchange farming for other work, their days turn to the dollar rather than the sun. Some Amish businessmen I interviewed seemed harried by new economic elements. A peaceful lifestyle was being eroded by business demands that their sophistication could handle but that their traditions could not. How can one run a self-sustaining enterprise in the twentieth century without a car and a phone? Some Amish leave the Old Order strand and throw themselves into a more liberal branch. Others cooperate with non-Amish to meet their business needs.

The tensions of living a nineteenth century mode and pace in the twentieth century burden some Amish. There are few structures to deal with the mental health needs that arise from new stresses. And avenues for growth exist only within prescribed boundaries. A person can receive training beyond the Amish School, but only by correspondence.

Amish life may seem idyllic, but its well-being may suffer from misinformation and ignorance. The absence of basic health understanding makes some Amish vulnerable to preventable diseases. It is sad for a child to acquire lockjaw or other diseases that vaccines can prevent.

As a people, the Amish face the future rather than shrink from it. Those who are willing to be philosophical about themselves point to family respect as the source of Amish strength. As offspring honor the ways of their parents, the generational cycle goes on with promise. They call it "keeping the faith."

The Amish Way

Previous pages: lush eastern Lancaster County is home for 15,000 Old Order Amish people. A long Amish funeral procession jags along Newport Rd. near Intercourse from the home of the deceased to Myers Cemetery for the burial. The farmstead (right) has been the hub of the Amish's family and church life since they settled in fertile Lancaster County in the 1720s. Visiting neighbors and relatives in the family vehicle, a gray carriage (below), gives children experiences that firm their place as Amish. These youngsters enjoy an excellent rear view from the buggy on a warm evening, while oldsters relive their younger days of travelling in the open "courtship buggy" (below right).

Previous page: Amish children grow up gaining responsibility in caring for the homestead. Martin bird houses stand in the yards of many Amish farms. Opposite page: Amish children learn early independence in the outdoors (top left); the value of farm upkeep, such as a well-painted fence row (center); road safety (bottom), and inventive ways of waiting and horse-watching (right). Left: a young Amish girl takes in the antics of an auctioneer at a sale to benefit the Bareville Fire Co., a community affair that her people wholeheartedly support. Below: a young man manages an errand on his own scooter, while (bottom) younger pre-schoolers at play in the safety of their driveway mimic harnessing, a routine Amish skill.

Far left: from infancy, children go with their parents, here in arms with a wagon in tow behind the pony cart transporting the needed bassinette. Bottom left: a custom-made carriage serves as an Amish station wagon with room for picnickers, the chairs and food for an outing. Children are expected to work. A Saturday task may be washing the nylon-covered carriage (left) in preparation for Sunday, or picking a bouquet of chrysanthemums (bottom center) for the parlor. Amish children ingeniously mix work and play. Below: these use draught power to lighten the task of mowing the lawn at their home along Irishtown Rd. Hitching, harnessing and riding are Amish play activities that become adult routines. Bottom: young adventurers, one on scooter and two on foot, move the family carriage across the driveway, likely a coveted chore.

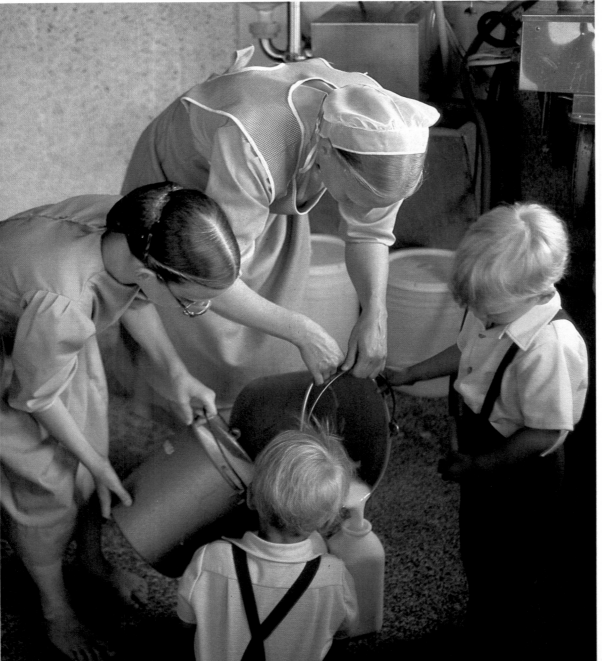

From their earliest days Amish children absorb the value of caring for the creatures of the earth and the environment that supports them. Above left: a young girl demonstrates an ease with animals along the country roads of eastern Lancaster County. Farm life affords Amish children many chances to feed, groom and tend livestock and pets. Above: eating a cool watermelon, a well-deserved break from the tiring job of cutting tobacco leaves. On a hot, humid summer day children do their part in the strenuous field work. Amish children learn to work by watching and helping those who are older. Left: five-year-old twins wait for their mother and sister to fill bottles of milk to feed the calves on their family dairy. The youngsters will have assistance until they can do the chore independently. Opposite page: in the company of a parent, an Amish child securely encounters the non-Amish or "English" world away from the homestead – along the road, in stores, at auctions or repair shops. A questioning child learns what is "our way" or *unserer weg* in Pennsylvania Dutch, the language of their community.

School Days

Opposite page: (top) during recess and dinnertime Amish children, Grades 1-8, play outdoors if the weather permits. While the younger pupils engage in High Water, a rope game, the older girls watch, leaning against the protective shelter of the outhouse toilet. (Bottom left) the teacher reconvenes class in the one-room schoolhouse, a government concession to the Amish who feel that modern consolidated schools would be a negative influence on their offspring. (Bottom right) a skate to school along Amish Road is faster than the usual walk. Top left: the youngest in this family enjoys a wagon ride as all five scholars hustle home, about a mile and a half from school. The eldest boy carries a baseball glove. Top right: prisoners' base, an active tag game, is a favorite during recess at school. Above: dressed in the black outerwear that distinguishes their religious group, Old Order Amish children head homeward *en masse*. They carry lunch pails, baseball bats and gloves. Chores no doubt await them.

Previous pages: a wood-stove, wooden desks with inkwells, a line stretched for hanging fly paper in summer and mittens in winter, adorn one-room Musser School in session. With eight grades in one room, each row is usually a class. While the first graders practice their letters at the board, the teacher works with another class, and the older pupils study. The curriculum covers basic reading, writing and math skills. Amish schools today resemble the one-room community public schools most American children attended two generations past. Above: Amish schoolchildren and their teacher relish baseball and stretch the season as long as possible, playing in early spring and into late fall. Left: boys wear hats, straw in summer and black felt in winter, just like Amish men. At the age of nine, Amish girls pin a belted apron to their dresses instead of wearing pinafores.

Previous page: at the landmark age of 16, Amish youth begin "running around", which means joining a group or "supper gang". These young men travel to theirs for a Sunday evening singing. Dating is allowed at this age, but many Amish youth spend two or more years socializing with the "gang" before a boy singles out a specific girl and asks her for some private weekend time. Right: a dating couple in Sunday garb travel in the open buggy that is often a young man's first. Black attire on this young lady indicates that a relative recently died. Below: a group of girls walk across the pasture to join other youth. Young women usually prepare for the singing and catch up on neighborhood news while the boys play an outdoor sport. Opposite page: at this "supper gang" gathering, the young men tied their net to their buggies to play volleyball. Later the females may serve a treat of lemonade and pretzels or perhaps pizza, a favorite.

Amish society derives strength from age group associations. Within a "supper gang" youth who turn 16 the same year form a "buddy bunch", with potentially close friendships that continue into adulthood. Opposite page: two youth stride along Eby Road in Lancaster County to reach the Amish family hosting their "supper gang". Top left: other youth arrive by buggy, sometimes travelling as far as 20 miles, a two and a half hour journey, to be with the "supper gang" that they decided to join. Top right: females are as competent as males at handling a horse-drawn vehicle. In same-sex groups of girls, having personality is important for developing friendships. The "supper gangs" provide time for youth to relate outside the family but within the community. Above: the dresses, aprons and prayer coverings these girls are wearing were made in their own households, possibly by themselves.

Opposite page: in the shirts and vests made by their mothers these Amish youth anticipate an evening with their peers. The society tolerates some variant behavior during the "running around" years before a youth joins the Church, often a move that coincides with marriage. Below: youth sport baseball uniforms and layered haircuts at Sunday night softball competitions they have arranged with another Amish group. Bottom left: an Amish youth may decorate his buggy with such accessories as a radio or ornaments that reflect his personality. Bottom right: Amish buggies park at a farmstead and horses graze in the meadow, while most youth socialize and sing indoors on a summer Sunday evening. The choruses that the youth sing have a livelier tempo than the ancient hymns sung during preaching on Sundays, but the words are often in German. Some young people create new songs, teaching them to the others without accompaniment.

On a typical Amish wedding day, a Tuesday or Thursday during post-harvest November, carriages park (below) at the home of a bride during the all-day service and feast. An unmarried youth in a carefully brushed dress suit (right) and two young women in their best (bottom) exemplify the garb of Amish guests. "Gifts for the corner" (bottom right) are brought by friends and gradually put on the table during the afternoon singing. The bride passes finger sweets among the guests, keeping the containers for her new home. Opposite page: social times with neighbors, friends and relatives precede dating and marriage, usually after the age of twenty.

Previous page: during the bi-weekly Sunday morning preaching service at a member's home, an array of parked carriages announce the location of church in this district. The Amish share an Anabaptist heritage with the Mennonites, who also came to Pennsylvania for religious freedom. The Hans Herr House (above), the medieval Germanic-style home of a Mennonite bishop built in Lancaster County in 1719, offers visitors the European background of these two groups. The *Martyr's Mirror* (right), a book commonly found in Amish homes, documents persecution in Europe of Anabaptists. Opposite page: at the Ephrata Cloister, also in Lancaster County, a Protestant communal society was established in 1732, the same period Amish settled in the area. The kitchen work shows the simple lifestyle of Cloister sisters. Overleaf: Amish faith embodies the values of simplicity and nurture. A farmer works long and hard, using simple technology to nourish the earth for his own family and future generations.

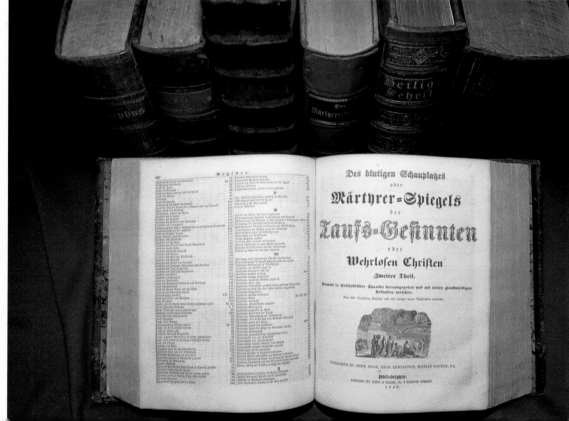

Dress regulations and other lifestyle practices comprise the *Ordnung*, unwritten rules of church order. They are based on Biblical principles and develop an Amish identity. At a public affair such as an auction (left), women wear the long-sleeved dress, black apron and pointed cape appropriate for older married Amish women in Lancaster County. Below: broadfall trousers with buttons instead of zippers are among the clothes hanging to dry on a typical laundry day. A mother sews her family's year-round wardrobe, being careful that the outerwear meets church regulations. Velcro is a modern product now used for fastening clothes, but some Amish cling to the traditional hooks and eyes. Opposite page: (top) this black buggy used by Amish in Mifflin County, PA, illustrates that practices vary with groups and areas. (Bottom) hooks for hanging clothes replace closets and curtainless windows mark an Amish home. Children's clothes are miniatures of their parents'. The white organdy apron and cape (bottom right) are worn to church.

Top: the Amish homestead provides a setting for group worship, weddings and funerals. Old Order Amish learn to read German, the language of their Bible, the *Ausbund* hymnal, and the *Christenpflicht*, a prayer book (left). Above: a leader leaves for church early Sunday morning. Ministers and bishops wear the usual Amish garb, serving without special training. Opposite page: residing in ordinary communities, the Amish remain separate; for example, their homes are not hooked up to the electric grid.

A windmill (left) and the absence (bottom) of electric wires at these Amish farms illustrate their desire to remain apart from the world. Amish feel that avoiding the source of power rules out the temptation to use it for forbidden entertainment. The New Testament in German (below), as translated by Martin Luther during the Reformation, is found in many Amish homes. Alongside their simplicity lies a work ethic that grooms their surroundings to enhance God's creation. Bottom: celosia flowers rim a vegetable garden with vibrant reds and yellows.

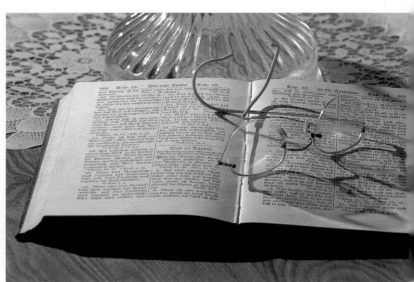

Previous page: rows of flowers, ageratum and marigolds, edge an Amish family's produce garden. A housewife uses a hand cultivator to clear unsightly weeds. The Swiss-German background of the Amish nudges them to utilize everything. During butchering they use meat scraps by making fresh and smoked sausage and bologna (opposite page top). They also enjoy ham, bacon and cheeses. Cup cheese (in front of the sausage stuffer – center) is usually served to spread on homemade bread at the fellowship meal after each Sunday preaching service. With boards to triple its length, the oilcloth-covered kitchen table (opposite page bottom left) is the center of family activities. Here the females peel garden produce and the family eats; under the propane gas lantern overhead members read or write letters. Opposite page bottom right: plain and fancy characterizes this Amish parlor with its wallpaper instead of the usual shiny painted walls. Fancy dishes, hand-painted wooden chairs, homemade throw rugs over woven rag carpets and crocheted doilies decorate a room saved for company. The rounded stool was made by covering tin cans. Left: this cookstove heats the kitchen of an Amish farmhouse in winter. A fitted dust cover drapes it during the summer. Amish brides nowadays still like a woodstove in their kitchens; their homes lack central heating. Below: this Amish can cellar shows how housewives preserve their garden surplus for off-season use. Overleaf: (left) a *grosdaddihaus* provides separate but connected living quarters for three generations. The additions built onto the original brick home in the center enable newlyweds and aging parents to be part of the life of the farm. (Right) a veterinarian's exam of a cow with milk fever interests three generations at this Amish farm.

Opposite page: the farm home is a place to enjoy pets. Top: schoolchildren help to milk at dawn, while preschoolers feed the calves later (left). Above: a boy pedals his wagon beside the family carriage during an early morning journey on Route 340 near White Horse. Overleaf: mist guards a farm along Newport Rd., Leola, in pre-dawn glow.

On farms averaging 55 acres, a farmer often does fieldwork within sight of the barn and house (below). Besides superb cultivation of the lawn and garden (bottom) by the women, the men fertilize according to soil needs (bottom center left). The milk man is one of the regular non-Amish visitors to the farm. Amish dairies store their milk over Sunday for Monday pickup (right). Neat, well-painted farmsteads (bottom center right), and mules (bottom right) resting on Sundays.

To make corn silage a team of 4-6 mules pulls a cutter that hoists the stalks onto a wagon (top left and left). To gather ear corn, a mule-drawn motorized picker plucks off the ears and drops them into a wagon pulled by another team (far left). Top: a frugal farmer teaches his young daughter to gather ears left by the picker. The iron-wheeled tractor (above) is used for stationary power. Overleaf: helpful with fieldwork, children haul alfalfa hay.

Opposite page: (top) a summer sunset bathes a Lancaster County Amish farm as evening fieldwork ends. An Amish farm owns at least six horses and mules to pull field implements for cultivation (bottom). Feeding them year-round is a cropping consideration. With careful planning and cooperative weather as well as family help, a farmer may be able to harvest four cuttings of alfalfa each season. Raking and baling hay is a team effort (top). Left and above: a couple's cooperation brings in as many haybales as possible before sunset. Overleaf: an early summer view across Lancaster County from Scenic Drive shows field patterns that change each season. The Amish practice crop stripping and rotation to maintain soil quality.

Opposite page: although unpopular for its backbreaking nature, the group chore of weeding tobacco (top) offers time for competitive games and talk. (Bottom and right) when tobacco is ready for cutting, able-bodied members of all generations help to shear off the heavy stalks and spear the long green leaves on 48-inch lathes. Each full one, weighing up to 25 pounds, is lifted and hung on a specially built wagon (above and top) to be taken to the tobacco shed. Overleaf: a snack brought from the house breaks up the long, arduous days of "getting the tobacco in".

Top: even in the depths of dusk, a farmer works at harvesting the corn crop. The bounty of sour cherries (above) to can for pie-baking and apples (right) to boil into sauce or dry as snitz delight both picker and housewife. Opposite page: a family may head for a pick-your-own orchard at the strike of dawn. Overleaf: (left) while autumn browns the earth, tobacco also dries, hanging from ceiling to floor, soaking sun and air. With training and muscle development, workhorses (right top) may gain in value for a few years, while a tractor depreciates. (Right bottom) at sunset a young boy leaves the field for home.

Amish farmers consistently work in their fields, taking time off only for rain, funerals and an occasional trip. Opposite page: buggies converge at this farmstead for a funeral. An Old Order Amish farmer uses less commercial fertilizer because he has more manure to spread on his fields. The Amish feel that their horse-drawn cultivation aerates rather than compacts the soil, improving drainage. After corn harvest comes fertilizing (this page).

Winter weather does not keep the Amish at home. Above: a horse treads easily along Snakehill Road near Leola through snowdrifts, and the narrow carriage wheels do not get stuck. In a household with no central heating, chopping firewood (right) for the woodstove is an essential fall chore. Opposite page: the productive Lancaster County soil lies fallow under winter's snow cover. Blankets, wool or fur keep Amish winter travelers warm inside an enclosed carriage (top). (Bottom) an Amish boy in an everyday winter cap awaits the mail at the end of the lane. The cold increases Amish dependence on letters for communication because visiting is more difficult. While the land rests, the Amish farmer strips and grades tobacco leaves and repairs equipment for the next growing season.

Horse-drawn transportation encourages Amish to live near each other. Such proximity enables Amish and other plain sects to experience community. Top center: barnraisings and other group volunteer projects express mutual care. Although Amish do not participate in government, they abide by laws that do not conflict with their religious principles. They show respect for the larger non-Amish community, often driving their slow-moving buggies at the side of busy Route 340 (left). Top: uphill travel is slow but the average speed is 10 mph on a main route. Above: letters are a link to other Amish settlements.

Amish donate time and goods to benefit disaster services. The Gordonville Fire Co. quilt sale (top left) and the Bareville Fire Co. auction (left) support community organizations that the Amish depend on year-round. Barn fires are a dreaded occasional reality in the Amish community. Amish groups also travel to other parts of the U.S. to help to rebuild after floods, hurricanes and other natural disasters in non-Amish communities. Above: Amish explore the wonders of a fire engine, and work closely with non-Amish at a benefit auction (opposite page bottom). Property sales attract Amish, some for bidding and others for visiting. Opposite page top: a downpour at one auction drove attenders to shelter on the wraparound porch.

Previous pages: country roads provide the
easiest route for Amish travel (left top), and even
a safe pause to chat with friends (left bottom).
Some fieldwork, such as baling alfalfa hay,
requires solitary concentration (right). Opposite
page: a family occasionally stocks up on food
staples that are not grown or preserved at home.
After a visit to an Amish grocery store, one girl
checks out the corn curls, a popular snack.
Amish-owned stores often sell general
merchandise, a convenience to their clientele.
Bulk purchases accommodate large family needs
and reduce time-consuming trips. Right: Amish
travelers along Route 340 near Intercourse
shield themselves from a surprise shower.
Below: in Intercourse to buy some household
goods, an Amishman carefully leads his horse
into the busy stream of traffic. A young family
member does her own checking from the
carriage window.

Left: an Amish couple travels together, perhaps to the home of a relative to spend a day on a work project that is lightened with more hands. Amish rely on the bus (below) or hired taxis to get to jobs off the farm – housework, waitressing or standing at market. Bottom: boys drive their pony cart along the main street of Intercourse, PA. Opposite page: a constable regulates traffic so that a carriage-drawn hearse can safely lead a funeral procession.

tercourse, PA.

Are The Amish?"
Amish World
azel's People"
Book and Craft
Shoppe

Above: Church Amish women quilt – a creative pastime. Besides quilting for family needs and sideline earnings, these members of a mission-minded Amish church prepare bedcovers for needy groups in the U.S. and abroad. Left: an Amish boy mows the lawn of his suburban home. The scarcity of affordable farmland and their high population growth rate have led some Amish into non-farm occupations and suburbia. The outside appearance of an Amish suburban ranch home may be nearly identical to a non-Amish home except for the green window shades. Opposite page: families gain seasonal income by taking surplus produce to market (top) or by selling it from their own roadside stand (bottom). Selling from the farm gives children opportunities to observe outsiders.

Left: two Amish men return from a day of non-farm wage work. Until they reach 21, children hand their earnings over to their parents, who supply their needs, including a furnished home upon marriage. Below: cottage industries owned by Amish meet the needs of their own community, but also serve non-Amish. Amish businesses such as this ice cream-producing dairy (bottom) employ their own people. This Church Amish-owned enterprise uses electricity. Opposite page: some Amish who do not farm engage in carriage repair and building.

Useful Beauty

Amish often express beauty in utilitarian objects; many have gained appeal among non-Amish buyers. Above: once made only for family use, Amish quilts flap from lines in Lancaster County to attract potential buyers. Far left: a traveler picks out a handcrafted item at a roadside stand. For additional income, Amish women craft discards and scraps into decorative items (left) for sale to tourists who travel to Lancaster County to see Amish country. Opposite page: a Church Amish craftsman, Isaac Kauffman, installs works into a chime clock to sell in a shop on his home property. Amish prefer to keep their work and family life as close as possible.

A Church Amish sculptor and painter, Aaron Zook (opposite page), makes his living contracting murals of Amish life scenes. Top: quilting at their monthly sewing circle gives the women of Weavertown Amish Church time to socialize and to quilt and sew dozens of items for relief. Amish make appliqued designs like the disselfink bird (left) to sell, but prefer pieced top quilts like this antique Lone Star pattern (above) for themselves.

Other Plain Folk

Mennonites subscribe to varying degrees of plainness. The Old Order Mennonites are known for driving teams. At a barnraising (above) near Honeybrook, PA, Amish join Old Order Mennonite men to put up a hip roof in one day. Top right: in light-colored suspenders and their Mennonite-style hats, the men watch the risky nailing of cross supports, while women observe from the yard (right). Far right: the balanced strength of many bodies raises the first rafters. Overleaf: within the overarching and surrounding elements of a secular society are people who dress plain and live in ways that mark their belief in God and separateness from the world. Raising the young in a way that will help them choose to stay in the church is a parental priority.

Later Years

Opposite page: (top) with grandparents living close by, Amish children learn from their experienced wisdom and enjoy their companionship. (Bottom left) a gray cape and wide-brimmed bonnet characterize an Old Order grandmother. The Amish accept and explain death, "The Lord giveth; the Lord taketh away." (Bottom right) family members remain at the gravesite until the earth is mounded over the opening. Above: before two funerals, members of the church district dig graves in Myers Cemetery. Simple, granite markers show other Amish burial sites. Amish society gives respect, honor and a meaningful place to the aged (right).

Amish funeral and burial practices in the Lancaster area follow a standard. It is customary for church and family members to perform many of the services that non-Amish accept from the funeral director. As soon as a body is embalmed, it is returned home. (Above) after a viewing and service on the main floor of the house, friends and relatives follow the body to an Amish cemetery. In the open air, members again view the deceased and then gather around the grave for a simple burial service (left). Opposite page: the last carriages of a funeral procession approach the cemetery for final farewells by family and friends. The fenced cemeteries are situated among the Amish farmlands.